# THE CHRISTMAS STORY

## IN STAINED GLASS

Photographs by Sonia Halliday
and Laura Lushington

**William B. Eerdmans Publishing Company**
Grand Rapids, Michigan

Centuries before the time of Christ,
God made a promise to his people:

'"The virgin will be with child
and will give birth to a son,
and they will call him Immanuel"
— which means, "God with us."'

That promise was fulfilled
in the birth of Jesus.
It came about in this way:

God sent the angel Gabriel to Nazareth, a town in Galilee, to a virgin pledged to be married to a man named Joseph, a descendant of David. The virgin's name was Mary. The angel went to her and said, 'Greetings, you who are highly favoured! The Lord is with you.'

LUKE 1:26-28

The angel brings God's message to Mary; the 'Annunciation', from Bourges Cathedral, France, fifteenth century.

Mary was greatly troubled at his words and wondered what kind of greeting this might be. But the angel said to her, 'Do not be afraid, Mary, you have found favour with God. You will be with child and give birth to a son, and you are to give him the name Jesus. He will be great and will be called the Son of the Most High. The Lord God will give him the throne of his father David, and he will reign over the house of Jacob for ever; his kingdom will never end.'

'How will this be,' Mary asked the angel, 'since I am a virgin?'

The angel answered, 'The Holy Spirit will come upon you, and the power of the Most High will overshadow you. So the holy one to be born will be called the Son of God. Even Elizabeth your relative is going to have a child in her old age, and she who was said to be barren is in her sixth month. For nothing is impossible with God.'

'I am the Lord's servant,' Mary answered. 'May it be to me as you have said.' Then the angel left her.

LUKE 1:29-38

Mary responds to the angel's message; a twelfth-century French panel showing the 'Annunciation', at Rivenhall, Essex, England.

At that time Mary got ready and hurried to a town in the hill country of Judah, where she entered Zechariah's home and greeted Elizabeth. When Elizabeth heard Mary's greeting, the baby leaped in her womb, and Elizabeth was filled with the Holy Spirit. In a loud voice she exclaimed: 'Blessed are you among women, and blessed is the child you will bear! But why am I so favoured, that the mother of my Lord should come to me? As soon as the sound of your greeting reached my ears, the baby in my womb leaped for joy. Blessed is she who has believed that what the Lord has said to her will be accomplished!'

LUKE 1:39-45

Mary greets Elizabeth; a sixteenth-century 'Visitation', at Notre Dame, Chalons-sur-Marne, France.

In those days Caesar Augustus issued a decree that a census should be taken of the entire Roman world. (This was the first census that took place while Quirinius was governor of Syria.) And everyone went to his own town to register.

So Joseph also went up from the town of Nazareth in Galilee to Judea, to Bethlehem the town of David, because he belonged to the house and line of David. He went there to register with Mary, who was pledged to be married to him and was expecting a child.

LUKE 2:1-5

Mary and Joseph on their way to Bethlehem; Chalons-sur-Marne, France, AD 1527.

While they were there, the time came for the baby to be born, and she gave birth to her firstborn, a son. She wrapped him in strips of cloth and placed him in a manger, because there was no room for them in the inn.

LUKE 2:6-7

The nativity; a fourteenth-century
German panel in the church of
St Étienne, Mulhouse, now in France.

And there were shepherds living out in the fields near by, keeping watch over their flocks at night. An angel of the Lord appeared to them, and the glory of the Lord shone around them, and they were terrified. But the angel said to them, 'Do not be afraid. I bring you good news of great joy that will be for all the people. Today in the town of David a Saviour has been born to you; he is Christ the Lord. This will be a sign to you: You will find a baby wrapped in strips of cloth and lying in a manger.'

LUKE 2:8-12

The angel appears to the shepherds; a French panel from about AD 1540 now in St Mary's Church, Stoke d'Abernon, England.

$\mathcal{S}$uddenly a great company of the heavenly host appeared with the angel, praising God and saying,

'Glory to God in the highest, and on earth peace to men on whom his favour rests.'

LUKE 2:13-14

Angels and shepherds; a nineteenth-century window by Burne Jones at Allerton, England.

When the angels had left them and gone into heaven, the shepherds said to one another, 'Let's go to Bethlehem and see this thing that has happened, which the Lord has told us about.'

So they hurried off and found Mary and Joseph, and the baby, who was lying in the manger. When they had seen him, they spread the word concerning what had been told them about this child, and all who heard it were amazed at what the shepherds said to them. But Mary treasured up all these things and pondered them in her heart. The shepherds returned, glorifying and praising God for all the things they had heard and seen, which were just as they had been told.

LUKE 2:15-20

Ａfter Jesus was born in Bethlehem in Judea, during the time of King Herod, Magi from the east came to Jerusalem and asked, 'Where is the one who has been born king of the Jews? We saw his star in the east and have come to worship him.'

MATTHEW 2:1-2

The Magi follow the star; a thirteenth-century panel in the 'Poor man's Bible' window at Canterbury Cathedral, England.

When King Herod heard this he was disturbed, and all Jerusalem with him. When he had called together all the people's chief priests and teachers of the law, he asked them where the Christ was to be born. 'In Bethlehem in Judea,' they replied, 'for this is what the prophet has written:
''But you, Bethlehem, in the land of Judah,
are by no means least among the rulers of Judah;
for out of you will come a ruler who will be the shepherd of my people Israel.'' '

Then Herod called the Magi secretly and found out from them the exact time the star had appeared. He sent them to Bethlehem and said, 'Go and make a careful search for the child. As soon as you find him, report to me, so that I too may go and worship him.'

MATTHEW 2:3-8

The Magi before Herod; thirteenth century, Canterbury Cathedral.

After they had heard the king,
they went on their way, and the star
they had seen in the east went ahead of
them until it stopped over the place
where the child was. When they saw the
star, they were overjoyed. On coming to
the house, they saw the child with his
mother Mary, and they bowed down and
worshipped him. Then they opened
their treasures and presented him with
gifts of gold and of incense and of
myrrh.

MATTHEW 2:9-11·

The Magi present their gifts; a
thirteenth-century panel in the
Bible window, The Three Kings
Chapel, Cologne Cathedral,
Germany.

And having been warned in a dream not to go back to Herod, they returned to their country by another route.

MATTHEW 2:12

God speaks to the Magi in a dream; thirteenth century, Canterbury Cathedral.

**W**hen the time of their purification according to the Law of Moses had been completed, Joseph and Mary took him to Jerusalem to present him to the Lord (as it is written in the Law of the Lord, 'Every firstborn male is to be consecrated to the Lord'), and to offer a sacrifice in keeping with what is said in the Law of the Lord: 'a pair of doves or two young pigeons.'

Now there was a man in Jerusalem called Simeon, who was righteous and devout. He was waiting for the consolation of Israel, and the Holy Spirit was upon him. It had been revealed to him by the Holy Spirit that he would not die before he had seen the Lord's Christ. Moved by the Spirit, he went into the temple courts. When the parents brought in the child Jesus to do for him what the custom of the Law required, Simeon took him in his arms and praised God, saying:
'Sovereign Lord, as you have promised, you now dismiss your servant in peace. For my eyes have seen your salvation, which you have prepared in the sight of all people,
a light for revelation to the Gentiles and for glory to your people Israel.'

LUKE 2:22-32

The 'Presentation' in the temple; by Ghiberti, AD 1445, the Duomo, Florence, Italy.

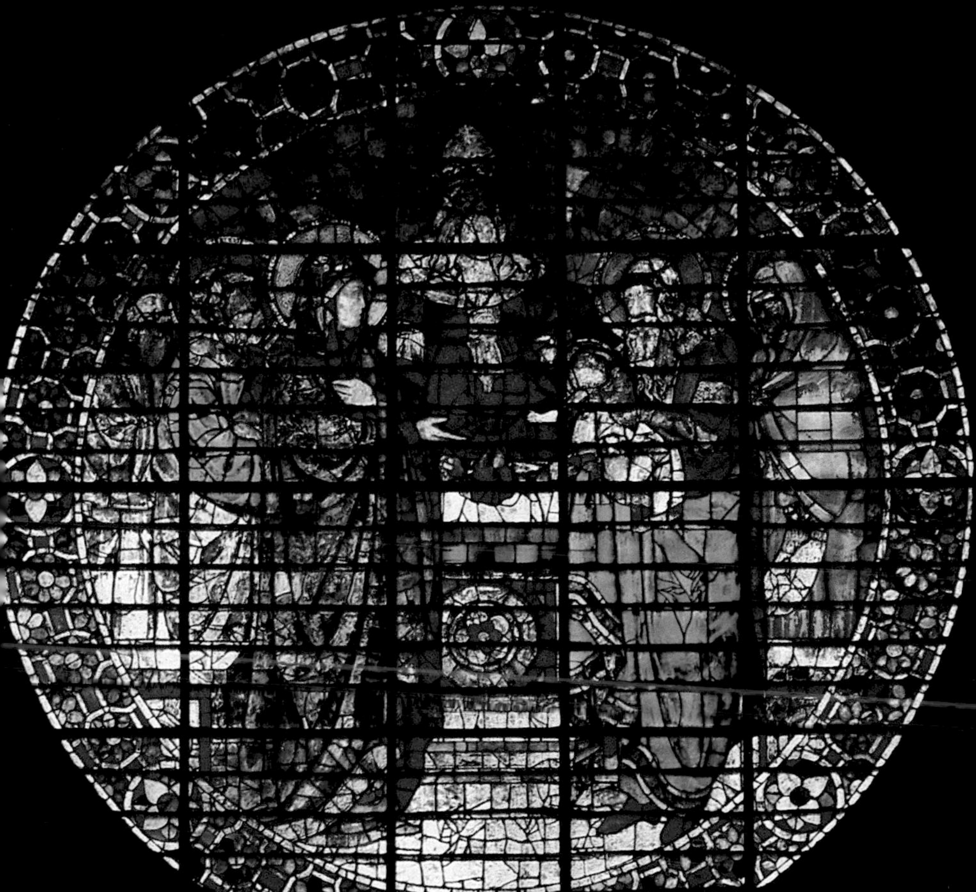

There was also a prophetess,
Anna, the daughter of Phanuel, of the
tribe of Asher. She was very old; she had
lived with her husband seven years after
her marriage, and then was a widow
until she was eighty-four. She never left
the temple but worshipped night and
day, fasting and praying. Coming up to
them at that very moment, she gave
thanks to God and spoke about the
child to all who were looking forward to
the redemption of Jerusalem.

LUKE 2:36-38

A nineteenth-century version of
the scene in the temple, at
Chesham, Bucks, England.

# T

he Word became flesh and lived for a while among us. We have seen his glory, the glory of the one and only Son, who came from the Father, full of grace and truth.

JOHN 1:14

After the Magi left, God warned Joseph that Herod wanted to kill Jesus. The family fled to Egypt until the danger was over. This seventeenth-century Swiss roundel is in the Church of St Peter and St Paul, Temple Ewell, Kent, England.

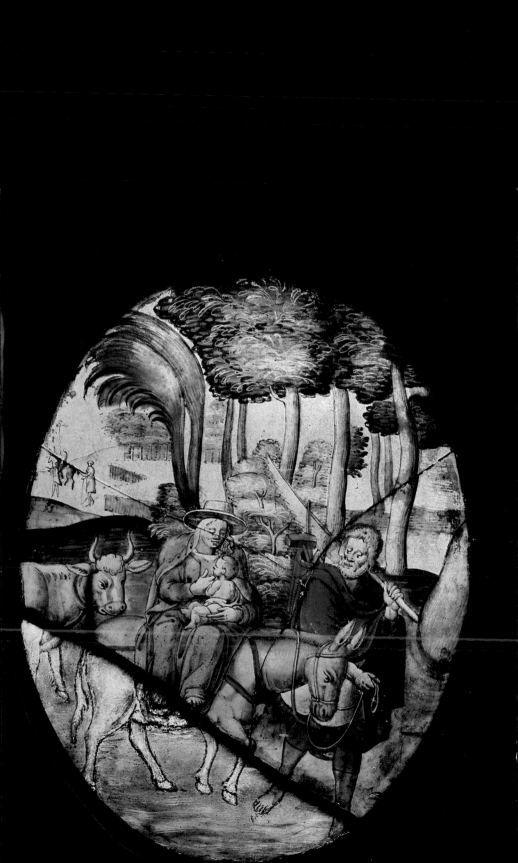

First published 1980 by Lion Publishing

First American edition published 1980 through
special arrangements with Lion by Wm. B. Eerdmans
Publishing Co., Grand Rapids, Michigan 49503.
ISBN 0-8028-3534-1

Copyright © 1980 Lion Publishing
First edition 1980
Photographs copyright © 1980 Sonia Halliday
Photographs; all photographs were taken on Pentax
6×7 equipment
Scripture quotations from the Holy Bible, New
International Version: copyright © New York
International Bible Society, 1978

Printed in Singapore by Toppan Printing Company Ltd